SITTING
ON A
ROCK

SITTING
ON A
ROCK

Gary L. Brinderson

BELLE ISLE BOOKS
www.belleislebooks.com

ISBN: 978-1-962416-18-4
Library of Congress Control Number: 2024900710

Designed by Sami Langston
Project managed by Leah Erwin
Cover art by Jennifer Wu

Printed in the United States of America

Published by
Belle Isle Books (an imprint of Brandylane Publishers, Inc.)
5 S. 1st Street
Richmond, Virginia 23219

BELLE ISLE BOOKS
www.belleislebooks.com

belleislebooks.com | brandylanepublishers.com

Contents

It's Still with Us

A storm does not stop being a storm
when it passes.
Childhood does not stop being childhood
when you become an adult.
Being in love does not stop the love you experienced
when you move on.
Education does not stop being a part of you
when you leave school.
Your favorite sport does not stop being a sport you favored
when you stop playing it.
A poem does not stop being a poem
after it touches your heart and mind.
History is the distance we have traveled.

Strength

Showing up,
strength has a large presence,
a quiet power,
a patience,
and a gentleness.
But it knows when to raise the white flag.

Thought

Any thought of love
that is transformed to action,
no matter how small—a hand on a shoulder,
a warm hug—
is perfect.

Mistake

Forget your mistakes,
but remember what they taught you.
Embrace the lesson,
and release the teacher.
Experience what is left after you make a mistake.

The Forest

When grief enters the forest,
there are several paths worth pondering.
There is only one path that leads to healing.
It's one foot in front of the other.

Mind

Our mind is an insane relative.

The feelings we have are real.

The story our insane relative creates is truthless.

I have named mine Homer.

I cut my foot.

Homer says, "You will bleed to death."

The bandage says, "No big deal."

Homer is very outspoken on everything we do.

Remember the feeling is real.

Receiving Love

How we observe others treating themselves matters:
with love and compassion,
or not,
with warmth,
or not,
with serenity,
or not.

It tells us how they will receive love.
Loving ourselves
like our best friend,
like our children,
like our favorite relative,
teaches others how to love us.

Three of Us

Our child:
If triggered, stomps their feet
and lets their feelings grow big;
They project them onto whoever triggered them.

Our teenager
who taught us to survive, any way that was necessary,
whatever our environment dictated.

The adult, who
on occasion
is calm, rational, logical, kind, and optimistic.

What's Unsaid

The elephant in the room
is always where needed knowledge lies.
Courage and heart can reap this field
and bring out the uncomfortable issues
that everyone has been avoiding.
But it needs to be understood.
It's like looking through a hole
in a castle wall,
where what is seen
is not spoken.

Left Behind

Achievement

has unintended consequences.

Our desire to grow means we leave others behind.

We have a choice: reaching back and staying connected or not.

The person left behind will not reach forward!

Recognizing Kindness

Affirmation.

Is it the smile,

the twinkling eyes

the open arms,

the gestures,

the words,

the energy,

the attention,

touch,

just being present?

Human connection.

Choose your magic to raise the spirits of others

while nourishing your own soul.

Mystery

This is the mystery of feeling hurt.
The whole body responds:
the pit in the stomach hardens,
the heart hurts.
What is the origin?
Is it from the experience at hand?
Or from my past?
From my mind?
The feelings are real,
but the mind creates stories that are false.
Are we assuming bad intentions towards us?
This is the mystery of feeling hurt.

Romantic Love

It has the power of the sea, wind, and fire combined.

You've never experienced so much power.

It brings happiness beyond our comprehension.

It changes our being as we know it.

It becomes all-consuming and joyous.

Our taste buds explode from the smallest taste.

We can smell the scent of a flower across the room.

A single note in a love song brings us to tears of joy and longing.

Love will bring you around the world to experience it for an hour;

you will think about it for hundreds of hours.

To experience its touch,

you will search for years.

To experience its feel,

you will be possessed.

To have its full embrace,

you will become unstoppable.

Seeing

When we become interested in something,
it becomes fascinating.
Do we see with our eyes
or with all our senses?
Do we see the object
or do we see the essence of the object?
Do we see things
or the surroundings of things?
Do we see the individual
or do we see the state of the individual?
Do we see the person
or their presence, their stature, their power?
Seeing has many dimensions.
When we overcome our biases
and add smell, taste, hearing, feelings, and intuition:
Now we are starting to *see*.

Need

At the center of human need is love.
To practice loving ourselves
is to let judgement fade away.
Loving others and loving to love others
will bring it full circle.
Being loved feels like home,
no matter where you are.
But loving others is the ultimate joy.

Imperfection

Sometimes we need to unlearn
what we believe.
Perfection is a lonely place.
Approachability versus isolation—
what is really appealing?
Perfection is a lonely place.
Imperfection is approachable.
Is perfection what we really want?
Looking in the mirror can be an affirmation.
Sometimes we need to realize what is really beautiful.

Nostalgia

Looking back:
Our first feelings of being in love,
infatuation.
Our first feelings of deepest love,
oneness.
Our first feelings of a true friend,
soul mate.
Our first feelings of being included,
part of.
Our first feelings with our pet,
unconditional love.
Our first feelings of caring for someone else's well-being,
full heart.
Our first feelings of a positive outcome from our efforts,
affirmed.
Our first feelings of conquering an intellectual challenge,
enlightened.
You can learn to become anything,
and if you grow, you can understand anything.

Our Legacy

Reflecting on our life—

what we have felt and given—

love stands out as the strongest feeling.

Experiencing our first romance.

Holding our first baby.

Hugging our best friend.

Caring for a loved one.

Could love be what our legacy really is?

Kindness

Our heart is in charge.
Start by being kind to yourself.
If we accomplish this consistently,
the act of being kind to others will become a natural reflex.
Kindness is frosting on the cake.
People only eat cake for the frosting.

Forgiving

One of the most liberating and selfish acts we can ever do
is to forgive someone.
We are doing this for ourselves,
not for them.

Sunshine

If you're lucky enough to be in love,
take it out for a walk on the beach in the sunshine.
Take it to see the full moon.
Take it to a friend's house.
Love likes to be celebrated.

Parents

We did not choose our parents,

but we can choose to define them by what we most admire.

All parents are flawed, as we are.

Understanding who they've become can be found

in their childhood, and their young adulthood.

The best source is their mom and dad,

uncles and aunts, brothers, and sisters.

The most important criteria to reflect on is,

did they do the best they could?

If they did, hold on to that.

If not, forgiving them is a terrific gift to yourself:

Not forgiving is drinking poison

and believing you're going to kill the other person.

Walk of Shame

When we let ego enter the room.

When our listening skills are not giving the other person what they deserve.

When we overlook the opportunity to be kind and caring.

When we accidently hurt someone.

When we miss an opportunity to give a compliment.

When we don't live up to our commitment, no matter how small.

When we judge others.

When we don't have the courage to do the right thing.

Partner

Loving to love doesn't leave room for judgment.

The dedication to love another takes all our senses to feel alive,

which enables us to understand the other person's needs and wants.

Being able to meet these is pure joy.

It keeps the relationship in a state of bliss.

What We Retain

What stays with us are the memories,
developed by feelings from the heart.
Our heart is the center of our being.
What is expressed may be uplifting or not,
but the feeling is what triggers the memory.

Line in the Sand

If we never become angry,
we never have to forgive
or draw a line in the sand.
As humans, maybe we can just erase the line.

Appreciation

Those who have had hardships
and disappointments
can most accurately describe
when they have had the feeling of being alive
in every cell of their being.

Listen

Listen to the universe.
It's saying the love invested in the world around you
will come back to you.

Whatever love you desire,
the universe has the person
that is longing to grace you with that love.

Let the universe work its magic.

What You Become versus Whom You Become

Formal education has you
focused on what you become:

a doctor,
a lawyer,
a carpenter,
a teacher,
an artist,
a scientist,
a salesperson.

Whom you become is ten times more important.
This is left to family, religion, tradition, or your own search for meaning.
Whom you become is your choice:

kind,
warm-hearted,
caring,
empathetic,
loving,
centered,
peaceful,
trusted,
good,
cheerful,
sweet.

The privilege of your journey is to decide whom you become.

Loss

Can you invite the imposter to dinner?
Will you accept loss as part of the journey
and let go?
Will you cherish the memories
or become victim?
Will you stand tall and strong
or shrivel back
and miss the opportunity
to embrace the renewal and birth of something new?
Will you be an example of growing
or be a martyr?
Only the opportunity to experience it
will write the ending.

Perseverance

Lean into the fire.

Perseverance is a motto for life.

Never, never give up no matter how much strife.

In family,

in friendship,

in education,

in work,

in every way,

in every area,

in every minute of every day.

Control the thoughts,

the outlook,

and where you want to go.

Comparison

Will we feel better about ourselves if we have that?

A material possession

A look

A degree

A bank balance

A vacation

A vocation

A partner

Comparison is a zero-sum game.

The winner of the game treasures what they have

Dressed

In our twenties, our outfits are what we think people want us to wear.

In our thirties, our outfits are what we want to become.

In our forties, our outfits are what's in style for our place in our culture.

In our fifties, our outfits present our comfort with ourselves.

In our sixties and beyond, our outfits are what lets us be comfortable.

Casting Who You Allow in Your Picture of Life

Choosing our life partner is the biggest decision we will ever make

and, like choosing our closest friends, creates the forum that dictates

the richness of our life's journey.

It's all in the casting!

Doors

When a door closes,

there are open doors all around us.

Our inner self sees them;

our mind tries to tell us they are an illusion.

Be courageous,

and walk through them.

Love

We forgot about love today
because we were mourning the past
and worrying about tomorrow.

Trust

It's earned over a long period
of small favors
carried out in ways that demonstrate
our confidence is placed in good hands.
It grows to the level of believing
our interest in this person's hands
comes before their own.
This is the ultimate honor system.

The Front Page

The facts never get in the way of a good story.

So, is all reporting just fiction?

Reminds me of gossip that's gone around the room

and is now on

the front page.

Preparation

When we are ready to leave our home,
how do we guide the restless
call of our ambition?
Our ear to the ground, testing opportunities.
We will find our deepest need can be filled
by being of service to others.

Dream

When a dream appears
and is yours for the taking,
loosen your grip on anything
that can get in its way.
Hold tight to your dream
with both hands.

Intentions to Grow

Our heart requires us to shed the things
in our life that weigh us down.
This opens up space;
we are able to free the heart,
to dream of other ideas to step into.
Don't let the mind talk you out of taking the step!
If you do the opportunity will dissolve into thin air.

Gut

The gut knows things the mind misses.

The body knows things the gut and the mind miss.

The heart knows things the mind, the gut, and the body miss.

Celebration

Our highest level of being
becomes apparent to ourselves
when we feel elated for another
person's successes.

Thoughts I've Only Shared with You

How feeling unworthy affects our ability to dream.

How the need for love underlines life itself.

How the heart is the center of our universe.

How a soulmate changes our existence.

How kindness to others does more for us than the recipient.

How loving to love keeps us feeling alive.

How treating ourselves as our best friend is beneficial for anyone we come in contact with, including ourselves.

How shedding judgment is like learning to see.

Failure

Failure is part of life's journey.

It does not represent who a person is.

It represents the results of a task.

What is done with that information is the opportunity.

Of course, the obvious is to improve and grow,

but for some the obvious is missed.

It is also a time to observe our emotions,

our ability to rationalize,

to gain humility and empathy,

to observe where things went wrong

and commit not to repeat it,

to set a new, smarter path,

to be more strategic,

to ask questions of ourselves

that we wouldn't have asked before.

Our senses are raised;

that wouldn't have been without the failure.

Failure is a stepping stone to higher levels of success

without arrogance and with empathy.

Now with confidence in knowing we are not dependent

on having only success in our life,

we move towards being a better person.

A failure is an opportunity to grow,

and show your character in getting back up.

We all fall down.

It's the ultimate test.

Without it,

we're not whole.

Embrace the lesson, release the teacher.

Heart

Wearing our heart on our sleeve
is one of the most courageous things we do!
We have learned to hide our heart, but
love has the ultimate power.
Penciling over in the blank spaces will always feel best.
Being in our heart is a choice.
When we're there the world looks completely different,
and the world looks back at us in a completely different way.
We were created to be in our heart.
Start looking.
Look in the eyes of a three-year-old.
That's where the wisdom of love lies:
the unknowing.

The Long Way

If it's raising a child,
learning a language,
playing an instrument,
mastering a sport,
overcoming a trauma,
there are no shortcuts.
No CliffsNotes,
no skipped chapters,
no silver bullets.
No passing the baton,
just perseverance.
There is only one foot in front of the other.

Path

When we enter life and look around for directions,
we see the vastness of different paths.
We realize then that the only perfect path
is one of our own making.

A Friend

The foundation of the soul lies in friendship,

a space reserved for acceptance and humble honesty,

a feeling of being understood wherever we may be on life's
journey,

a connection that reaches beyond continents and seas.

It is always with us even if we have time apart.

That feeling of serving, nurturing,

and observing wisdom being built,

one experience at a time,

is tremendously fulfilling.

Knowing we are someone's safe harbor,

and fully trusting they are ours,

is one of life's ultimate longings.

Cherish your friends.

They are life's true treasure.

Loneliness

A feeling we all dread.

It can be when we are within

a swarming city, with our closest friends, in a crowd,

or in solitude.

Is it our reality?

Or of our own mind?

The feeling is real!

If we are kind in our heart,

and reach out to others with a helping hand,

this feeling will transform into compassion.

Compassion for self and others comes back.

Power of Misfortune

Misfortune has no power.

We give it power.

It can become a teacher,

or it can become a tragedy.

Misfortune given power

creates a victim.

Hurt Grows

Hurt unresolved grows and magnifies
When damage is done, restoration is mandatory
The memory of hurt is forever if not rectified
Apologies and forgiveness are kissing cousins

Adolescence

Trying to find your place!

From comfort,
warmth,
connection to Mom—
the nourishment of her energy and love,
the safety and protection—
to unchartered waters,
loss of connection,
self-doubt,
not being perfect,
not being enough,
the little body changing,
no one saying why.
When will it stop?
Separating from Mom is happening slowly,
but always continuing.
The world is hard
when you are in
the in-between.

Fear

Fear is the opposite of love.

Love is the emotion we want to enjoy a long, hot bath in,

with bubbles,

and be transformed.

Fear is what goes down the drain.

Awareness of Spaces

Life has spaces that give us the opportunity to bring
different elements of our being into action
to have the richest experience.

A space for execution of a task,
a space for a passion—
a high-level sport,
an art—
a space for reflection at forty thousand feet,
or planning the future,
a space for deep connection with a friend or a child,
a space for romantic love and intimacy,
a space for spirituality,
a space to learn and experience.

Be aware of what space we are in,
and understand elements of one's self that we are required to
draw upon to maximize the experience.

Courage

Approach is soft and gentle.

Speaking from your heart is brave.

Delicacy is manliness.

Humility is vulnerability.

Empathy is gallantry.

Kindness is caring in a competitive world.

Something for Everyone

When we are looking at the eyes of a friend or child,
with love in our hearts,
a smile or nod of the head,
the message is *affirmation*.

Affirmation, even so small,
creates a good feeling in the recipient,
as well as the affirmer.
The same expressions given to a baby,
bring a giant smile or laugh.
Or to a child, think of
the adolescent who really needs to be affirmed.
Affirmation is like oxygen.
From something as small as a smile to,
"You are the best person I have ever met,"
We have so many opportunities. There are no limits.
It starts in the mirror,
and goes to infinity.

That's Love

Her head on your shoulder
That look of adoration
Eye contact that's locked in for what seems like hours
That helping hand that's always there
The overuse of *I love you*
Encouraging words at every talk
The compliments from the heart
That feeling of being cherished
Always feeling that you're number one
Watching the sun go down together
Bringing coffee to the other in bed
Sending a love poem
Your awe when she walks in the room
You look so beautiful
The excitement of knowing you have uninterrupted time
together
The pride that comes from knowing she loves you
The feeling of being deeply loved

Written Word

It can warm a heart to the level of bringing a tear.

It can inflict pain that can last a lifetime.

It goes much farther and to corners we don't realize.

It has a bigger shadow than we can see.

It can come from love and land softly.

It can come from fear and land like a wrecking ball.

It's all at the tips of our fingers.

Spaces

There are different spaces in life,

and we are completely different people in each one.

Fight or flight,

totally consumed.

Reflective,

calm mind and quiet.

Completing a task,

focused.

Doing a sport that you're passionate about,

elated and challenged.

Listening to another person,

being consumed with all your senses and heart.

Be aware of the space you're in at all times,

and be in the right state of mind for each.

You Are

Much more than you believe
You are the most beautiful woman on the planet
You are Madison Avenue
You are intuition
You are the one with the best heart
You are the light in the cloud
You are sensuality

Problems

Problems are everywhere.
When we are pondering them,
envision goodness—it's there!

Flowers

A person in love's senses are on high alert.

They can appreciate beauty from across a room,

and detect an exotic scent when entering a space.

Flowers send a message of love,

through beauty of colors and shapes,

that illuminate a room and bring an array of emotions.

A fragrance that can bring tears.

Brighten Our Light

One of the biggest gifts we can give ourselves
is the ability to accept
with no judgement.
This is a very tall order
but an extraordinary accomplishment
towards enlightenment.

Judging others is a defense,
counter to love and compassion,
that we need for ourselves
to brighten our light in the world.

Universe

The universe, in its mysterious way,
perpetuates the dreamer's dream.

The Journey

How do we enrich the journey?
Being true to who we have become,
treating ourselves as we would our best friend.
Openess and empathy lead to understanding
for ourselves and others.
Growing feeds the heart,
allowing it to become more open,
to let love come in.

Insight

We never forget the people who saw something great in us in our darkest moments.

Transformation

The gift a student brings is their time, attention,
and desire to learn and grow.
The student's dream is to enter a space where they feel special,
listened to, and not judged,
which frees their mind to explore the new,
to be challenged using their mind and heart,
to have knowledge come in a unique form.
It opens their minds to a new way to think,
when it's delivered with a humble, human heart.
Their life is changed.

Feelings to Live By

To looking into the eyes of the love of your life.

To laughter.

To seeing your love enter a space and fill your heart with joy.

To the elation of a passion.

To the safe harbor of your soulmate.

To the glow of a child's face that feels love.

To observe someone
who has found an answer to a life struggle.

To the greeting of a friend that you love.

To watching your child become the person they are.

To the feeling of growing as a person.

To the joy of loving to love.

To helping another person grow.

To observing someone close to you fall in love.

Tears

Our tears' story,

is it here and now?

Or from the past?

Is it singular?

Or multiple hurts?

Ignited from our exterior?

Or from within?

Is it our child?

Our survivor?

Our adult?

Fear is always the invader.

The level of excruciation

is commensurate to our trauma.

The Feeling of Elation

Your voice will go up a notch,

you express elation,

your excitement becomes contagious,

your mind becomes singularly focused,

you go from routine to a child at play,

where time does not exist,

where your soul is alive!

You feel heaven is close by.

Following the Heart

Being fearless,
taking one step,
can change your life
like magic.

Success

Success comes from our life's experiences,

and an imaginary place that we believe to be true.

In Cuba, success is a number just over the poverty line.

In Fiji, it means being a part of the community

(Fiji Island is one of the happiest places on Earth).

In America, the imaginary place continues to move.

We are always living in the future,

which steals from the present and our ability to be content.

Success is whatever you describe it to be.

Living in the present and being at peace with who we are,

and where we are on our journey,

is key to contentment.

Realize that happiness is a choice.

Contentment and contemplation give us the insight

to see that success is our own imaginary will.

Choose

Choose love over:

Winning

Being right

Debate

Drinking

Being important

Tears

Anxiety

Hate

Bitterness

Losing

Anger

Partying

Duty

Politics

What others want

Love should be pervasive

Brothers and Sisters

We have our brothers and sisters.

We choose our friends.

We have our family.

Our brothers and sisters have the same frailties as our best friends.

We have an opportunity to treat them the same
and commence a lifelong journey of fulfillment.

This is a choice.

Even if the love is not returned,

being a caring brother or sister

is one of life's highest gifts.

Compartments

Putting parts of our lives into compartments is a skill
that keeps the subject clear and takes less voltage.
Each compartment has its own importance;
the most important one is our own inner self.
It must be held dear
and never depleted.

Small Talk

Talking about people makes us feel EMPTY.

Talking about events makes us feel GOOD.

Talking about ideas makes us feel EXCITED.

Talking about service to others makes us feel COMPAS-SIONATE.

Confuse

Don't confuse quiet
with peace.
Don't confuse beauty
with a good heart.
Don't confuse strength
with character.
Don't confuse intellect
with wisdom.
Don't confuse education
with perseverance.
Don't confuse infatuation
with being in love.

Connection

Where is our safe harbor?

We only have a few,

but we know with whom.

There is no judgment.

They know what a mess we are

and love us unconditionally.

Cherish them.

They are wonderful.

Stay focused on keeping them alive and well.

With them we have a space that is warm and safe,

like a hot bath.

Perfect

Don't hint I'm perfect.
Lying is unattractive.
Tell me I am a damaged,
insecure,
controlling,
hyperactive teenager,
but that's why you love me.

Counterintuitive

When we are putting something off,
we need to deal with it.
When there is an elephant in the room,
we need to address it.
When our partner pushes us away with harsh words,
we need to hold them.
When we want to send a difficult message,
sending it with love is a game changer.

Getting Through a Difficult Time

Invest love in others with listening,
Vulnerability, and transparency,
leading with our hearts.
This fills our need for caring
and fills our soul.
This wonderful feeling lets our bucket of love spill over.

When we're going through difficult times,
we take from our bucket by asking for help,
and give our friends the gift of filling their need to feed
their souls.
So accept those difficult times when they show up.
With no guilt, just accept their warmth.

The Ocean

The ocean brings us such a rainbow of emotions:
the peace that warms our hearts,
the delight in colors that bring a smile,
the vastness that we find hard to compare,
the freshness that makes our skin become sensitive,
the surrealness that lets our mind contemplate meaning,
and most of all,
the beauty that lets us appreciate our ability to love.

The Road to Misunderstanding

We see ourselves as our intentions.

Others see us as our actions.

Never assume—

always confirm the other person's intentions—

before you draw a conclusion.

Head Versus Heart

The heart listens to the head,
carrying on with great patience and admiration
for a while.
Then, the heart realizes
that the head is going to ruin the evening.

What are we to do with such misguided enthusiasm?

Connection to Nature

Vitamin N

Oceans

Mountains

Deserts

Wild Great Plains

Forests

Rivers

Cities

We connect with a space

that restores us with

renewed invigoration.

Definition of Friendship

Someone who cares for you *unconditionally*,
who knows, with no judgement, that you are a mess
(we are all a mess, just to varying degrees),
who has the right to tell you if you are doing something not
in your best interest.
But if you decide to do it,
they support you one hundred percent.

Love's Irreplaceable Things

Her smile

Her eyes

Her walk

Her laugh

Her sense of humor

Her touch

Her beauty

Her sensuality

Her style

Her insights

Her intuition

Her inner child

Her excitements

Her kisses

Her heart

Discover

We don't know what we don't know.
If we become interested in something,
it becomes interesting.
Accept what comes from silence.

Love's Moments

The bed turned down
Delivering coffee
Sending a poem
Opening a door
Delivering medication
Putting cash in a purse
Picking the colors and scent of a bouquet
Being barefoot together
The red sunset
The green flash
Sitting in a beautiful garden
Listening to the waves
A favorite love song
Laughter
Room service
Having white space to fill

Acceptance

Acceptance is the cornerstone of mental health.

Accepting ourselves with all our flaws is where the journey begins and ends. We have an opportunity every minute to accept, learn, and engage or reject and close our minds to other views.

The learning is always in the *why* and not in the *what*.

Openness to different ways of thinking, of improving our ways of listening. There is always more than one answer to an issue.

Looking in the mirror with total acceptance and love is one of life's biggest challenges.

Unconditionally accepting who we are—not what we want to become, not what society wants us to be, not what anyone else wants us to be—but who we are gives us the ability to grow.

Total unconditional acceptance of a friend is the first step of growth, and with that you start to be able to do it with your spouse, then your child; then you start to see, and the world looks different, more friendly, more tolerant. You see love in more places than ever before.

Mentoring

Mentoring is about helping a person to know themselves:

to manage themselves in the most effective way,

to stay centered,

to lead and to learn in their life challenges,

to have pride and enjoy their journey,

to feel good about the way they accept themselves and people they love,

to continue to put effort into all relationships that are important to them so that they feel good about themselves,

to feel good about the people they come in contact with,

to set their own goals and to have their own dreams,

to know their own drivers,

to be at peace with and know their own fears,

to have a passion in their life,

to take care of themselves physically so they can live life to the fullest,

to enjoy the ride (there is no station),

to keep the ego in check and to use their heart more,

to make timely decisions,

to learn fairness is the cornerstone of leadership,

to learn that forgiveness is for them, not for the person they are forgiving,

to learn the difference between the person's behavior and the person.

Finding the right answer within the mentee, for the mentee, is our role.

Giving the mentee options that the mentee hasn't thought about, helping them see beyond the present to a bigger universe and life journey.

Listening with a third ear, looking back to what you have learned over a period of time, keeping them true to who they are and what they want to become.

Just being there for them unconditionally without judgement can open their minds and help them express their own insights.

Cement

Love is the strongest relationship cement in the universe.

It's magic.

If it's not working,

start a mutiny by loving more.

History

We are not our traumas

We are the collective sum of how we overcame

Tell Me

Tell me you will put love above everything in your life.

Some days it will be hard.

We will have to stop and reflect:

Where does what we are doing really belong in our higher arc of importance?

There will be days of bliss where we are on top of the world, bathing in love.

Whatever we are doing, is love present?

Our heart is where we find the illumination of love.

This is where we find the best answers to life's most difficult questions.

Thank You

Thank you for seeing more in me than I was able to see.

Thank you for making me open to believing I am loved.

Thank you for letting me love you.

Thank you for reminding me to laugh.

Thank you for the best times of my life—being together.

Thank you for our hearts, so filled with love for each other.

Shit Storm

We have all been in the middle of a meltdown.
All our emotions are triggered:
Fight, flight, or freeze.
Calm says "This is not from what's happening.
It has activated something from the past.
It has nothing to do with me."
Calm is so wise.

The Outlier

There are rough diamonds that shine.

There are people whose word is unbreakable.

There are quiet people with the largest presence.

There is always one who is unstoppable.

There is one that is forever young.

The Right Path

When you're in your heart
When your mind is your best friend
When your body is in training to go the distance
When relationships are home
You have done all the heavy lifting
You're on the right path
Let yourself feel alive

About the Author

Gary L. Brinderson is the Chairman of Brinderson Holdings, with investments in institutional, industrial, multifamily real estate, software, transportation, and equities. Mr. Brinderson graduated summa cum laude with an MBA from Pepperdine University. He is also a graduate of the Advanced Management Program and an alumnus of Harvard Graduate School of Business. He chairs Leadership Fellows at the University of California, Irvine Paul Merage School of Business, and is past chair of the same program at HEC in Paris and NYU.